The Complete Legal Form Book
of Living Wills

by

Ernest Edsel, J.D.

ISBN 978-0-557-06320-8

The Complete Legal Form Book
of Living Wills

This is a public interest law book
of the
Folger Public Policy Research
Center on Death and Dying

Copyright (c) 2009 by Ernest M. Edsel

First Edition

Printed and Manufactured in the United States of America

ISBN 978-0-557-06320-8

The Complete Legal Form Book
of Living Wills

Table of Contents

Author

Ernest Edsel is a published attorney with more than 20-years experience, admitted to practice before state and federal courts in Washington and Texas

Publisher

This is a public interest law book of the Folger Public Policy Research Center on Death and Dying. The Center helps individuals understand and prepare for death. We do this by public policy research into living and dying with dignity, hope, and peace. And, we publish helpful books and papers on death and dying, including books with legal forms, such as advance directives to physicians.

PREFACE

This book is divided into four chapters. Each chapter has its own page numbering.

It's up to you, the reader, to decide which of the forms you want to complete, sign, and use.

As for living will forms, you must choose between Chapter One and Chapter Two because they are practically the same, except that Chapter Two is suitable if you have family members who might object to your healthcare decisions and end-of-life choices.

Below are brief descriptions of each chapter.

Chapter One is a living will form that contains a simple medical directive to physician and a medical power of attorney. This form is sufficient for most people.

Chapter Two is a living will form that contains a medical directive to physician (and family) and a medical power of attorney. This form was written for persons with family members who might object to your advance directives and other end-of-life healthcare choices.

Chapter Three is a pain and comfort management plan, which is a detailed plan that is not included in Book One and Two (although each of the directives in Book One and Book Two contain a clause directing doctors to provide drugs to eliminate pain, anguish, and/or agitation).

The Pain Management Plan is written for persons who do not know their doctors well enough to trust them to provide all necessary medicines to eliminate pain, anguish, an/or agitation in any end-of-life situation. The plan is also written for persons who do not trust their doctors and healthcare providers well enough to provide all necessary drugs to eliminate the agitation that often develops with many types of dementia.

Chapter Four has practical and comprehensive instructions and directives to leave for your loved ones in case of your serious illness or death. This form is extremely useful and recommended for everyone. The form includes a comprehensive checklist of practical matters that you need to consider and prepare for in the event of your serious illness or death. The chapter also contains a short list recommended books on death and dying.

After you pick between Chapter One and Chapter Two, I suggest that you copy the form and then write on that copy so that any mistake can be corrected by making another copy of the needed page from this book. The same "copy and write" principle applies if you decide to use the forms in Chapter Three and Four.

Each of the four chapters are sold separately as inexpensive and instant download e-books at:

http://stores.lulu.com/folgercenter

You can also read our blogs and connect with us at

www.folgercenter.blogspot.com

http://folgercenter.tumblr.com

www.folgercenter.wordpress.com

Thank you for getting ths book to protect yourself and loved ones.

Ernest Edsel, J.D.
The Folger Public Policy Research Center on Death and Dying

CHAPTER ONE:

Living Will Form (with instructions).

Contains two legal forms: a simple advance directive to physician; and, a medical power of attorney. Includes clause directing doctors to provide drugs to eliminate pain, anguish, and/or agitation.

ADVANCED DIRECTIVE TO PHYSICIAN

AND

MEDICAL POWER OF ATTORNEY

INTRODUCTION

This is my advanced directive to my physicians and healthcare providers. It is my express desire that my family and friends comply with and honor this directive.

I understand that I do NOT have to fill out and sign this form.

I have decided to fill out and sign the directive in order to control the type of healthcare that I receive in case of a terminal or life-threatening illness.

This directive also contains a medical power of attorney that names the individual who I am authorizing to make medical decisions for me in ANY type of disease or medical condition in the event that I am unable to make medical decisions as a result of a severe injury or any medical treatment that leaves me without the full mental capacity to make medical treatment decisions, including surgical decisions or the type of rehabilitation and therapy. I understand that I should choose a person, as my healthcare representative under the medical power of attorney, who has enough courage, determination, and intelligence to achieve the purposes of the advance directive to physician.

This document includes the signature of two witnesses on page 15. If I and the witnesses have the time and ability to do so, then we will get this document notarized on pages 18-19. This document is and remains legally binding even if we do not have the time or ability to complete the notarized section on pages 18-19.

This document also contains, in page 16, the signature of the person who agrees to serve as my health care representative.

I understand the importance of my health care providers knowing my wishes and preferences for my health care. Therefore, I am providing a copy of this completed and signed document to my health care providers, including the following doctor(s) and health care providers :

1._____ of _____;
   (name of doctor or medical provider)   (city, state)

2 _____
   (name of hospice/nursing provider, if applicable)

of _____;
   (city, state)

I will also consider if I will donate my organ and tissues as part of this directive on page 9.

ADVANCE DIRECTIVE

[NOTE: YOU DO NOT HAVE TO FILL OUT AND SIGN THIS FORM]

PART A: IMPORTANT INFORMATION ABOUT THIS ADVANCE DIRECTIVE

This is an important legal document. It can control critical decisions about your health care. Before signing, consider these important facts:

Facts About Part B (Appointing a Health Care Representative)

You have the right to name a person to direct your health care when you cannot do so. This person is called your "health care representative." You can do this by using Part B of this form. Your representative must accept on Part E of this form. You can write in this document any restrictions you want on how your representative will make decisions for you. Your representative must follow your desires as stated in this document or otherwise made known. If your desires are unknown, your representative must try to act in your best interest. Your representative can resign at any time.

Facts About Part C (Giving Health Care Instructions)

You also have the right to give instructions for health care providers to follow if you become unable to direct your care. You can do this by using Part C of this form.

Facts About Completing This Form

This form is valid only if you sign it voluntarily and when you are of sound mind. If you do not want an advance directive, you do not have to sign this form.

Unless you have limited the duration of this advance directive, it will not expire. If you have set an expiration date, and you become unable to direct your health care before that date, this advance directive will not expire until you are able to make those decisions again.

You may revoke this document at any time. To do so, notify your representative and your health care provider of the revocation.

Despite this document, you have the right to decide your own health care as long as you are able to do so.

If there is anything in this document that you do not understand, ask a lawyer to explain it to you.

You may sign PART B, PART C, or both parts. You may cross out words that don't express your wishes or add words that better express your wishes. Witnesses must sign PART D.

Print your NAME, BIRTH DATE AND ADDRESS here:

_____

(Name)

_____

(Birth date)

_____

(Address)

Unless revoked or suspended, this advance directive will continue for:

INITIAL ONE:

    _____   My entire life

    _____   Other period (_____ years)

PART B: APPOINTMENT OF HEALTH CARE REPRESENTATIVE

I appoint _____ as my health care representative.

My representative's address is _____ (City, State) and his/her telephone number is

_____ .

I appoint _____ as my alternate health care representative if my agent is unable or unwilling to make health care decisions for me.

My alternate's address is:

_____ (City, State) and telephone number is

_____ .

I authorize my representative (or alternate) to direct my health care when I can't do so.

If the persons designated as my agent and alternate are unable or unwilling to make health care decisions for me, I designate the following persons to serve as my agent to make health care decisions for me as authorized by this document, who shall serve in the following order:

Second Alternate Agent:

_____,
       (printed name)

who is my _____ (relationship);

Third Alternate Agent:

_____,
       (printed name)

who is my _____ (relationship).

NOTE: You may NOT appoint your doctor, an employee of your doctor, or an owner, operator or employee of your health care facility, UNLESS that person is related to you by blood, marriage or adoption or that person was appointed before your admission into the health care facility.

INITIAL below if you want your health care representative to obey your directive:

_____ My representative is to honor this Health Care Instruction or Directive to Physicians.

1. *Limits to this Directive.* List special conditions or instructions (if any):

_____

_____

_____

2. *Life Support.* "Life support" refers to any medical means for maintaining life, including procedures, devices and medications. If you refuse life support, you will still get routine measures to keep you clean and comfortable.

INITIAL BELOW IF THIS APPLIES:

_____ My representative MAY decide about life support for me. (If you don't initial this space, then your representative MAY NOT decide about life support.)

3. *Tube Feeding.* One sort of life support is food and water supplied artificially by medical device, known as tube feeding.

INITIAL BELOW IF THIS APPLIES:

_____ My representative MAY decide about tube feeding for me. (If you don't initial this space, then your representative MAY NOT decide about tube feeding.)

DATE AND SIGN HERE TO APPOINT THE HEALTH CARE REPRESENTATIVE LISTED ABOVE IN PAGE FOUR:

_____
(signature of person making appointment)

_____
(date of signing)

PART C: HEALTH CARE INSTRUCTIONS

NOTE: In filling out these instructions, keep the following in mind:

The term "as my physician recommends" means that you want your physician to try life support if your physician believes it could be helpful and then discontinue it if it is not helping your health condition or symptoms.

"Life support" and "tube feeding" are defined in Part B above.

If you refuse tube feeding, you should understand that malnutrition, dehydration and death will probably result.

You will get care for your comfort and cleanliness, no matter what choices you make. You may either give specific instructions by filling out Items 1 to 4 below, or you may use the general instruction provided by Item 5. Here are my desires about my health care if my doctor and another knowledgeable doctor confirm that I am in a medical condition described below:

1. *Close to Death.* If I am close to death and life support would only postpone the moment of my death:

    A. INITIAL ONE:

      __ I want to receive tube feeding.

      __ I want tube feeding only as my physician recommends.

      __ I DO NOT WANT tube feeding.

    B. INITIAL ONE:

      __ I want any other life support that may apply.

      __ I want life support only as my physician recommends.

      __ I want NO life support.

2. *Permanently Unconscious.* If I am unconscious and it is very unlikely that I will ever become conscious again:

    A. INITIAL ONE:

      __ I want to receive tube feeding.

      __ I want tube feeding only as my physician recommends.

      __ I DO NOT WANT tube feeding.

B. INITIAL ONE:

__ I want any other life support that may apply.

__ I want life support only as my physician recommends.

__ I want NO life support.

3. *Advanced Progressive Illness*. If I have a progressive illness that will be fatal and is in an advanced stage, and I am consistently and permanently unable to communicate by any means, swallow food and water safely, care for myself and recognize my family and other people, and it is very unlikely that my condition will substantially improve:

A. INITIAL ONE:

__ I want to receive tube feeding.

__ I want tube feeding only as my physician recommends.

__ I DO NOT WANT tube feeding.

B. INITIAL ONE:

__ I want any other life support that may apply.

__ I want life support only as my physician recommends.

__ I want NO life support.

4. *Extraordinary Suffering*. If life support would not help my medical condition and would make me suffer permanent or severe pain, anguish, or agitation:

A. INITIAL ONE:

___ I want to receive tube feeding.

___ I want tube feeding only as my physician recommends.

___ I DO NOT WANT tube feeding.

B. INITIAL ONE:

___ I want any other life support that may apply.

___ I want life support only as my physician recommends.

___ I want NO life support.

5. *General Instruction*.

INITIAL BELOW IF THIS APPLIES:

_____ I do not want my life to be prolonged by life support. I also do not want tube feeding as life support. I want my doctors to allow me to die naturally, and without pain or agitation, if my doctor and another knowledgeable doctor confirm I am in any of the medical conditions listed in Items 1 to 4 above. And, I want my doctors to provide me with drugs that eliminate pain, anguish, and/or agitation, in whatever necessary dosage, including non-opioid and opioid analgesics (including morphine), to eliminate my level of pain, anguish, and/or agitation and to use all other suitable classes of drugs, including barbiturates, benzodiazepines, corticosteroids, anti-convulsants, and other anti-anxiety and anxiolytic agents (including clonazepam).

6. *Additional Conditions or Instructions* (if any)(insert description of what you want done, including a "Do Not Resuscitate" order):

_____

_____

_____

_____

7. *Other Documents.* A "health care power of attorney" is any document you may have signed to appoint a representative to make health care decisions for you.

INITIAL BELOW to revoke any health care power of attorney made in the past:

_____ I revoke any health care power of attorney I have made in the past.

SIGN AND DATE HERE TO IMPLEMENT THE INSTRUCTIONS OF PART C

_____   _____

(signature of person making instructions)   (date)

- 13 -

PART D: ORGAN AND TISSUE DONATION

INITIAL ONE:

_____ I do NOT want to donate my body, organs, or tissues.

_____ I want to donate my entire body for medical use and study.

_____ I want to donate my organ(s) or tissue(s) and therefore direct that my tissues and organ be donated.

INITIAL ONE if you want to donate organs or tissues:

_____ any tissues and organs needed by any medical organization;

_____ ONLY the following tissues and organs:

_____

_____

PART E: DECLARATION OF WITNESSES

We declare that the person signing this advance directive:

(a)   Is personally known to us or has provided proof of identity;

(b)   Signed or acknowledged that person's signature on this advance directive in our presence;

(c)   Appears to be of sound mind and not under duress, fraud or undue influence;

(d)   Has not appointed either of us as health care representative or alternative representative; and

(e)   Is not a patient for whom either of us is attending physician.

Witnessed By:

_____   _____
(Signature of Witness/Date)   (Printed Name of Witness)

_____   _____
(Signature of Witness/Date)   (Printed Name of Witness)

NOTE: One witness must not be a relative (by blood, marriage or adoption) of the person signing this advance directive. That witness must also not be entitled to any portion of the person's estate upon death. That witness must also not own, operate or be employed at a health care facility where the person is a patient or resident.

PART F: ACCEPTANCE BY HEALTH CARE REPRESENTATIVE

I accept this appointment and agree to serve as health care representative. I understand I must act consistently with the desires of the person I represent, as expressed in this advance directive or otherwise made known to me. If I do not know the desires of the person I represent, I have a duty to act in what I believe in good faith to be that person's best interest. I understand that this document allows me to decide about that person's health care only while that person cannot do so. I understand that the person who appointed me may revoke this appointment. If I learn that this document has been suspended or revoked, I will inform the person's current health care provider if known to me.

_____

(Signature of Health Care Representative/Date)

_____

(Printed name)

PART G: ADDITIONAL DIRECTIVE

As for my funeral arrangements, I want the following if I have not donated my body to science:

INITIAL ONE:

_____ I want to be cremated.

_____ I do not want to be cremated and want to be buried without embalming.

_____ I do not want to be cremated and want to be buried with embalming.

PART H: SELF-PROVING AFFIDAVIT

```
THE STATE OF _____  }
                               }
COUNTY OF _____     }
```

BEFORE ME, the undersigned authority, on this day personally appeared

_____,

_____, and

_____, known to me to be the declarant and the witnesses, respectively, whose names are subscribed to the annexed or foregoing instrument in their respective capacities, and, all of said persons being by me first duly sworn,

_____, the said declarant, declared to me and to the said witnesses in my presence that said instrument is the declarant's medical power of attorney and advanced directive to physician and that the declarant had willingly made and executed it as declarant's free act and deed for the purposes therein expressed; and the said witnesses, each on their oath stated to me, in the presence and hearing of the said declarant, that the said declarant had declared to them that said instrument is the declarant's medical power of attorney and advanced directive to physician, and that the declarant executed same as such and wanted each of them to sign it as a witness; and upon their oaths each witness stated further that they did sign the same as witnesses in the presence of the said declarant and at the declarant's request; that the declarant was at that time more than eighteen (18) years of age and of sound mind; and that each of said witnesses was then more than eighteen (18) years of age.

Declarant: _____
                    (signature)

Witness: _____
                        (signature)

Witness: _____
                        (signature)

SUBSCRIBED AND ACKNOWLEDGED BEFORE ME by the said declarant and each witness on

this ____ day of _____, 200_____.

NOTARY SEAL

_____
(Notary Signature)

Notary Public

in _____County,

State of _____

For the State of _____

Printed Name of Notary:

_____

My Commission Expires:

_____

- 19 -

CHAPTER TWO

Living Will Form (with instructions).

Contains two legal forms: an advance directive to physician(and family); and, a medical power of attorney.

This form is best for persons with family members who might object to advance medical decisions for end-of-life healthcare. Includes clause directing doctors to provide drugs to eliminate pain, anguish, and/or agitation.

You need to choose a person, as your healthcare representative under the medical power of attorney, who has enough courage, determination, and intelligence to achieve the purposes of the advance directive to physician.

ADVANCED DIRECTIVE TO PHYSICIAN AND FAMILY

AND

MEDICAL POWER OF ATTORNEY

INTRODUCTION

This is my advanced directive to my physicians and healthcare providers. I understand that I do not have to fill out and sign this form.

I have decided to fill out and sign this directive in order to control the type of healthcare that I receive in case of a terminal or life-threatening illness. This directive also has a medical power of attorney appointing a representative to make medical decisions for me in ANY medical situation in which I may not have full mental capacity or ability to make medical decisions.

The medical power of attorney names the individual who I am authorizing to make medical decisions for me in ANY type of disease or medical condition in the event that I am unable to make medical decisions as a result of a severe injury or any medical treatment that leaves me without the full mental capacity to make medical treatment decisions, including surgical decisions or the type of rehabilitation and therapy.

This document includes the signature of two witnesses on pages 11-12 and 18. If I and the witnesses have the time and ability to do so, then we will get this document notarized (see pages 21-22). This document is and remains legally binding even if we do not have the time or ability to complete the notarized section on pages 21-22.

I understand the importance of my health care providers knowing my wishes and preferences for my health care. Therefore, I am providing a copy of this completed and signed document to my health care providers, including the following doctor(s) and health care providers :

1. _____
(name of doctor or health care provider)

of _____ (city, state);

2. _____
   (name of hospice/nursing provider, if applicable)

of _____ (city, state)

The original of this document is kept at:

_____
(address and location of the document inside that address)

MY ACKNOWLEDGMENT AS TO THE DIRECTIVE

I understand and know the following with respect to my advance directive:

1.   This is an important legal document known as an Advance Directive. It is designed to help me communicate my wishes about my medical treatment at some time in the future when I am unable to make my wishes known because of illness or injury.

2.   These wishes are usually based on personal values. In particular, I may consider what burdens or hardships of treatment I would be willing to accept for a particular amount of benefit obtained if I were seriously ill.

3.   I may discuss my values and wishes with my family or chosen spokesperson, as well as with my physician. My physician, other health care provider, or medical institution may provide me with various resources to assist me in completing my advance directive. Brief definitions are listed below to assist me in my discussions and advance planning.

4.   I will initial the treatment choices that best reflect my personal preferences.

5.   I will provide a copy of my signed directive to my physician, healthcare provider, usual hospital, and family or spokesperson.

6.   I will consider a periodic review of this document. By periodic review, I can best assure that the directive reflects my preferences.

7.   In addition to this advance directive, I am considering other directives that can be important during a serious illness. These include the Medical Power of Attorney (which is part of this document) and the Out-of-Hospital Do-Not-Resuscitate Order (which is a form that my doctor must sign). I may discuss these forms with my physician, family, hospital representative, or other advisers.

8.   I may also consider completing a directive as part of this directive that controls the donation of my organs and tissues.

MY ACKNOWLEDGMENT AS TO THE MEDICAL POWER OF ATTORNEY

I understand and know the following with regards to my medical power of attorney:

1.   Except to the extent I have stated otherwise in writing in this document, this document gives the person I name as my agent the authority to make any and all health care decisions for me in accordance with my wishes, including my religious and moral beliefs, when I am no longer capable of making them myself. Because "health care" means any treatment, service or procedure to maintain, diagnose, or treat my physical or mental condition, my agent has the power to make a broad range of health care decisions for me. My agent may consent, refuse to consent, or withdraw consent to medical treatment and may make decisions about withdrawing or withholding life-sustaining treatment. My agent may not consent to voluntary inpatient mental health services, convulsive treatment, psychosurgery, or abortion. A physician must comply with my agent's instructions or allow me to be transferred to another physician. My agent's authority begins when my doctor certifies that I lack the competence to make health care decisions. My agent is obligated to follow my instructions when making decisions on my behalf.

2.   Unless I state otherwise in writing, my agent has the same authority to make decisions about my health care as I would have had. I understand that it is important that I discuss this document with my physician or other health care provider before I sign it to make sure that I understand the nature and range of decisions that may be made on my behalf. If I do not have a physician, I understand that I should talk with someone else who is knowledgeable about these issues and can answer my questions. I do not need a lawyer's assistance to complete this document, but if there is anything in this document that I do not understand, I know that I should ask a lawyer to explain it to me.

3.   The person I appoint as agent should be someone I know and trust. The person must be 18 years of age or older or a person under 18 years of age who has had the disabilities of minority removed. If I appoint my health or residential care provider (e.g., your physician or an employee of a home health agency, hospital, nursing home, or residential care home, other than a relative), then that person has to choose between acting as my agent or as my health or residential care provider because the law does NOT permit such a person to do both at the same time.

4.   I should inform the person I appoint that I want them to be my health care agent. Also, I should discuss this document with my agent and my physician and give each a signed copy. And, I should indicate on the document itself the people and institutions who have signed copies.

5.   My agent is not liable for health care decisions made in good faith on my behalf.

6.   Even after I have signed this document, I have the right to make health care decisions for myself as long as I am able to do so and treatment cannot be given to me or stopped over my objection.

7.   I have the right to revoke the authority granted to my agent at any time by informing my agent or my health or residential care provider orally or in writing, by my execution of a subsequent medical power of attorney.

8.   Unless I state otherwise in writing, my appointment of a spouse dissolves upon any legal filing or proceeding for divorce or legal separation.

9.   This document may not be changed or modified. If I want to make changes in the document, I will make an entirely new one.

10.   I can designate an alternate agent in the event that my agent is unwilling, unable, or ineligible to act as your agent. Any alternate agent I designate has the same authority to make health care decisions for me.

11.   This Power of Attorney is not valid unless I sign it in the presence of two competent adult witnesses.

12.   The following persons may not act as a witness:

(a) the person I designate as my agent;

(b) a person related to me by blood or marriage;

(c) a person entitled to any part of my estate after my death under a will or codicil executed by me, or by operation of law;

(d) my attending physician;

(e) an employee of my attending physician;

(f) an employee of a health care facility in which I am a patient if the employee is providing direct patient care to me or is an officer, director, partner, or business office employee of a health care facility or of any parent organization of the health care facility; or,

(g) a person who, at the time this power of attorney is executed, has any claim against any part of my estate after my death.

ADVANCE DIRECTIVE

[NOTE: I KNOW THAT I DO NOT HAVE TO FILL OUT AND SIGN THIS FORM]

DIRECTIVE TO PHYSICIANS AND FAMILY OR SURROGATES

I recognize that the best health care is based upon a partnership of trust and communication with my physician. My physician and I will make health care decisions together as long as I am of sound mind and able to make my wishes known. If there comes a time that I am unable to make medical decisions about myself because of illness or injury, I direct that the following treatment preferences be honored, as follows:

1.   If, in the judgment of my physician, I am suffering with a terminal condition from which I am expected to die within six months, even with available life-sustaining treatment provided in accordance with prevailing standards of medical care, then:

INITIAL ONE:

_____ I request that all treatments other than those needed to keep me comfortable be discontinued or withheld and my physician allow me to die as gently as possible, without pain, anguish, or agitation;

_____ I request that I be kept alive in this terminal condition using available life-sustaining treatment. (THIS SELECTION DOES NOT APPLY TO HOSPICE CARE.)

2.   If, in the judgment of my physician, I am suffering with an irreversible condition so that I cannot care for myself or make decisions for myself and am expected to die without life-sustaining treatment provided in accordance with prevailing standards of care, then:

INITIAL ONE:

_____ I request that all treatments other than those needed to keep me comfortable be discontinued or withheld and my physician allow me to die as gently as possible, without pain, anguish, or agitation;

_____ I request that I be kept alive in this irreversible condition using available life-sustaining treatment. (THIS SELECTION DOES NOT APPLY TO HOSPICE CARE.)

3.   Additional requests (if any, including a "Do Not Resuscitate" order): (After discussion with your physician, you may wish to consider listing particular treatments that you do or do not want in specific circumstances, such as artificial nutrition, intravenous antibiotics, etc. Be sure to state whether you do or do not want the particular treatment.)

_____

_____

_____

4.   In the event that I or my representative elect hospice care after I sign this directive, I understand and agree that only those treatments needed to keep me comfortable would be provided and I would not be given available life-sustaining treatments.

5.   If any of my representatives are not available, or if I have not designated a spokesperson, I understand and request that under this directive a spokesperson be chosen for me following standards specified in the laws of my state.

6.   If, in the judgment of my physician, my death is imminent within minutes to hours, even with the use of all available medical treatment provided within the prevailing standard of care, then I acknowledge that all treatments may be withheld or removed except those needed to maintain my comfort.

7.   I understand that this directive has no effect if I have been diagnosed as pregnant.

8.   I want my doctors to provide me with drugs that eliminate pain, anguish, and/or agitation, in whatever necessary dosage, to carry out this directive.

9.   This directive will remain in effect until I revoke it. No other person may do so.

_____

(Signature)

(Printed Name) _____

Date:_____

City, County, and State of Residence: _____

Two competent adult witnesses must sign below, acknowledging the signature of the declarant. The witness designated as **Witness 1** may not be a person designated to make a treatment decision for the patient and may not be related to the patient by blood or marriage. This witness may not be entitled to any part of the estate and may not have a claim against the estate of the patient. This witness may not be the attending physician or an employee of the attending physician. If this witness is an employee of a health care facility in which the patient is being cared for, this witness may not be involved in providing direct patient care to the patient. This witness may not be an officer, director, partner, or business office employee of a health care facility in which the patient is being cared for or of any parent organization of the health care facility.

WITNESS DECLARATION

We declare that the person signing this advance directive:
(a)   Is personally known to us or has provided proof of identity;
(b)   Signed or acknowledged that person's signature on this advance directive in our presence;
(c)   Appears to be of sound mind and not under duress, fraud or undue influence;
(d)   Has not appointed either of us as health care representative or alternative representative; and
(e)   Is not a patient for whom either of us is attending physician.

Witnessed on this ___ day of _____, 2_____ by:

Witness 1:   _____
                   (Signature)

                   _____
                   (Printed Name)

Witness 2: _____
(Signature)

_____
(Printed Name)

Definitions:

"Artificial nutrition and hydration" means the provision of nutrients or fluids by a tube inserted in a vein, under the skin in the subcutaneous tissues, or in the stomach (gastrointestinal tract).

"Irreversible condition" means a condition, injury, or illness:

(1) that may be treated, but is never cured or eliminated;

(2) that leaves a person unable to care for or make decisions for the person's own self; and

(3) that, without life-sustaining treatment provided in accordance with the prevailing standard of medical care, is fatal.

Explanation: Many serious illnesses such as cancer, failure of major organs (kidney, heart, liver, or lung), and serious brain disease such as Alzheimer's dementia may be considered irreversible early on. There is no cure, but the patient may be kept alive for prolonged periods of time if the patient receives life-sustaining treatments. Late in the course of the same illness, the disease may be considered terminal when, even with treatment, the patient is expected to die. You may wish to consider which burdens of treatment you would be willing to accept in an effort to achieve a particular outcome. This is a very personal decision that you may wish to discuss with your physician, family, or other important persons in your life.

"Life-sustaining treatment" means treatment that, based on reasonable medical judgment, sustains the life of a patient and without which the patient will die. The term includes both life-sustaining medications and artificial life support such as mechanical breathing machines, kidney dialysis treatment, and artificial hydration and nutrition. The term does not include the administration of pain management medication, the performance of a medical procedure necessary to provide comfort care, or any other medical care provided to alleviate a patient's pain.

"Terminal condition" means an incurable condition caused by injury, disease, or illness that according to reasonable medical judgment will produce death within six months, even with available life-sustaining treatment provided in accordance with the prevailing standard of medical care.

Explanation: Many serious illnesses may be considered irreversible early in the course of the illness, but they may not be considered terminal until the disease is fairly advanced. In thinking about terminal illness and its treatment, you again may wish to consider the relative benefits and burdens of treatment and discuss your wishes with your physician, family, or other important persons in your life.

The phrase "drugs that eliminate pain, anguish, and/or agitation" means non-opioid and opioid analgesics (including morphine), to eliminate my level of pain, anguish, and/or agitation and all other suitable classes of drugs, including barbiturates, benzodiazepines, corticosteroids, anti-convulsants, and other anti-anxiety and anxiolytic agents (including clonazepam).

MEDICAL POWER OF ATTORNEY

Designation of Health Care Agent:

I appoint the following person:

_____
(name)

_____
(address)

_____
(telephone)

as my agent to make any and all health care decisions for me, except to the extent listed in the limitations section below.

This medical power of attorney takes effect if I become unable to make my own health care decisions and this fact is certified in writing by my physician.

Limitations On The Decision Making Authority Of My Agent Are As Follows (if I leave this section empty, then I want my agent to make any and all health care decisions for me):

_____

_____

_____

Designation of an Alternate Agent:

(Although not required to designate an alternate agent, I understand that I may do so, especially if my designated agent is far away, sick, and otherwise unwilling or unable to act.

I understand that the alternate agent may make the same health care decisions as the designated agent if the designated agent is unable or unwilling to act as my agent.)

(I also understand that if the agent designated is my spouse, then the designation is automatically revoked by law if our marriage is dissolved.)

I designate the following person(s), to serve as my agent to make health care decisions for me as authorized by this document, who shall serve in the following order:

First Alternate Agent:

Name: _____

Address:_____

Phone: _____

Second Alternate Agent:

Name: _____

Address:_____

Phone: _____

Duration

I understand that this power of attorney exists indefinitely from the date I execute this document unless I establish a shorter time or revoke the power of attorney. If I am unable to make health care decisions for myself when this power of attorney expires, the authority I have granted my agent continues to exist until the time I become able to make health care decisions for myself.

[*In the event that I want this medical power of attorney to last for a short time, then I hereby specify that this medical power of attorney shall end on the following date:*

the ____ day of _____, 2_____]

Revocation

I revoke any prior medical power of attorney.

Acknowledgment of Disclosure Statement

I have been provided, in pages 3-5, with a disclosure statement explaining the effect of this document. I have read and understand the information contained in the disclosure statement.

Signature and Date

I hereby sign my name to this medical power of attorney on

this _____ day of _____, 2_____ in

the _____ city/town in the State of

_____.

_____
(my signature)

_____
(my printed name)

Statement and Signature of First Witness

I am not the person appointed as agent by this document. I am not related to the principal by blood or marriage. I would not be entitled to any portion of the principal's estate on the principal's death. I am not the attending physician of the principal or an employee of the attending physician. I have no claim against any portion of the principal's estate on the principal's death. Furthermore, if I am an employee of a health care facility in which the principal is a patient, I am not involved in providing direct patient care to the principal and am not an officer, director, partner, or business office employee of the health care facility or of any parent organization of the health care facility.

Signature: _____

Printed Name: _____

Date: _____

Address: _____

Signature of Second Witness

Signature: _____

Printed Name: _____

Date: _____

Address: _____

PART G: ADDITIONAL DIRECTIVES

ORGAN AND TISSUE DONATION

INITIAL ONE:

_____ I do NOT want to donate my body, organs, or tissues.

_____ I want to donate my entire body for medical use and study.

_____ I want to donate my organ(s) or tissue(s) and therefore direct that my tissues and organ(s) be donated.

INITIAL ONE if you want to donate organs or tissues:

_____ any tissues and organs needed by any medical organization;

_____ ONLY the following tissues and organs:

_____

_____

_____

FUNERAL ARRANGEMENT

As for my funeral arrangements, I want the following if I have not donated my body to science:

INITIAL ONE:

_____ I want to be cremated.

_____ I do not want to be cremated and want to be buried without embalming.

_____ I do not want to be cremated and want to be buried with embalming.

SELF-PROVING AFFIDAVIT

THE STATE OF _____ }
                              }
COUNTY OF _____   }

     BEFORE ME, the undersigned authority, on this day personally appeared

_____,

_____, and

_____, known to me to be the declarant and the witnesses, respectively, whose names are subscribed to the annexed or foregoing instrument in their respective capacities, and, all of said persons being by me first duly sworn, _____, the said declarant, declared to me and to the said witnesses in my presence that said instrument is the declarant's medical power of attorney and advanced directive to physician and that the declarant had willingly made and executed it as declarant's free act and deed for the purposes therein expressed; and the said witnesses, each on their oath stated to me, in the presence and hearing of the said declarant, that the said declarant had declared to them that said instrument is the declarant's medical power of attorney and advanced directive to physician, and that the declarant executed same as such and wanted each of them to sign it as a witness; and upon their oaths each witness stated further that they did sign the same as witnesses in the presence of the said declarant and at the declarant's request; that the declarant was at that time more than eighteen (18) years of age and of sound mind; and that each of said witnesses was then more than eighteen (18) years of age.

Declarant: _____
                        (signature)

Witness: _____
                    (signature)

Witness: _____
                    (signature)

SUBSCRIBED AND ACKNOWLEDGED BEFORE ME by the said declarant and each witness on

this _____ day of _____, 200_____.

NOTARY SEAL

_____
(Notary Signature)

Notary Public in _____County, State

of _____

For the State of _____

Printed Name of Notary:

_____

My Commission Expires: _____

CHAPTER THREE

This detailed Pain and Comfort Management Plan makes doctors and other healthcare providers provide you with all drugs and medical treatments to eliminate pain, anguish, and/or agitation at the end of your life or during a serious illness.

The plan is specifically designed to avoid horrible situations where patients are left without adequate medicines to eliminate pain, anguish, and/or agitation at the end of their life.

The plan makes sure that a patient always has the right medicine, regardless of whether it is a weekday, weekend, holiday, or whether the patient is at a hospital, hospice, at home, or elsewhere.

Although this pain management plan is not included in any of the advance directives to physician found in this book, each of the directives do indeed direct your doctors and healthcare providers to provide you with all necessary medicines, in any dosage, to eliminate pain, anguish, and/or agitation during any end-of-life situation.

Use this plan if you do not trust your doctors and healthcare providers well enough to provide you with all necessary medicines, in any dosage, to eliminate pain, anguish, and/or agitation during any end-of-life or serious illness situation.

If your doctor(s) refuses to discuss this form or the issues in this form, then it is your right, as a patient (or as a representative under a medical power of attorney), to demand and get a new doctor.

Your doctor must sign and date this form for it to become effective. If your doctor(s) refuses to sign this form (or refuses to provide, or agree to provide, similar orders), then it is your right, as a patient (or as a representative under a medical power of attorney), to demand and get a new doctor.

PAIN AND COMFORT MANAGEMENT PLAN

This plan is for: _____

(printed name)

_____

(address)

_____

(address)

PURPOSE OF THIS PLAN

This pain and comfort management plan is between my healthcare providers and myself.

I am presenting this plan to my doctor(s) and other healthcare providers to in order prevent a situation whereby I may be left for days or hours without any pharmaceuticals and other medical means to control and eliminate pain, anguish, or agitation during any serious or terminal illness or any other situation described in my advance directive to physician.

If any of my doctors refuse to discuss, complete, or implement this or a similar written pain and comfort management plan, then I understand, as my legal right as a patient, that I can and should immediately ask for and obtain another doctor who is willing to provide adequate pain management.

In the event that my healthcare representative, appointed under my medical power of attorney, is making medical decisions for me, then my representative shall seek and obtain this or a similar written pain and comfort management plan.

I am providing a copy of this completed and signed document to my health care representative named in my medical power of attorney and to all my healthcare providers, including the following doctor(s) and health care providers :

1. _____
   (name of doctor or medical provider)

of _____ (city, state);

2. _____

(name of hospital or clinic)

of _____

(city, state);

3. _____

(name of nursing or hospice provider, if applicable)

of _____

(city, state);

4. _____

(name of my appointed healthcare representative)

of _____

(city, state)

PAIN AND COMFORT MANAGEMENT PLAN

Whereas I, the patient, have been diagnosed with a medical condition that falls within my advance directive to physician, it is my desire that my doctor(s) and other healthcare providers(s) have a written understanding with me as to all procedures and treatments that will eliminate my pain, anguish, and/or agitation at all times, regardless of whether I am in a hospital, hospice, at home, or elsewhere.

Therefore, I and my doctors and other healthcare providers agree that:

1.   I will be provided with all necessary prescriptions, pharmaceuticals, therapies, and other medical means to eliminate my pain, anguish, and/or agitation at all times, regardless of whether: (a) it is during or after regular business hours on weekdays, a weekend, or a holiday; (b) I am in a hospital, a hospice, at home, or elsewhere.

2.   This plan will be shared among all my physicians, nursing and/or hospice staff, and all other healthcare providers.

3.   I will be constantly evaluated for: (a) pain, anguish, and/or agitation; (b) the type and level of the intensity of such pain, anguish, and/or agitation; and, (c) the effectiveness of all measures taken to eliminate pain, anguish, and/or agitation.

4.   If pain, anguish, and/or agitation are known, typical, or chronic symptoms of my disease or condition, then all necessary palliative and preventive measures shall be taken in advance before I begin to suffer pain, anguish, and/or agitation; thus, my healthcare providers shall implement all measures necessary to constantly maintain appropriate levels of medication at all times to prevent pain, anguish, and/or agitation.

5. First and foremost, my statements or indications of pain, anguish, and/or agitation will be taken as true. Second, all statements concerning my pain, anguish, and/or agitation by my healthcare representative, appointed under my medical power of attorney, will be taken as true. Lastly, statements concerning my pain, anguish, and/or agitation by any member of my family or circle of close, loved ones, will be taken as true.

6. All cause or causes of pain will be eliminated when possible.

7. I will be provided with analgesics and adjunctive modalities according to an appropriate and established pain rating scale criteria, such as the Wong-Baker Scale, Numerical Scale, and FLACC (face, legs, activity, cry, consolability) Scale.

8. I will be provided with all necessary non-opioid and opioid analgesics (including morphine) to eliminate my level of pain, anguish, and/or agitation as well as other suitable classes of drugs, including barbiturates, benzodiazepines, corticosteroids, anti-convulsants, and other anti-anxiety and anxiolytic agents (including clonazepam).

AGREED TO BY MY DOCTOR:

_____
(signature)

_____
(printed name)

_____
(date)

CHAPTER FOUR

The legal form in this chapter contains your *Final Instructions and Directives* in the event of a serious or terminal illness. The form also contains a comprehensive checklist of practical matters that you need to consider in the event of your death. Once you complete the form, it will be extremely valuable to anyone who has to manage your affairs after your death or while you are seriously or terminally ill.

Some pages have been left in blank to leave you extra room to write in important information. If you need to tape additional pages into the form, then number the additional page with alphabet letters. For example, suppose you want to add and tape two extra pages to page 5 (and each of the two extra pages have writing on the front and back of each page). In that case, you would then number the additional written pages, as follows: "5-A", "5-B", "5-C", and "5-D".

After completing the form, please make a copy and leave that copy with: (1) one or more close, trusted loved persons; and, (2) the person(s) who will handle your property and estate as your executor under your will.

If you have not named an executor in a written will, it's now a good time to get a will. There are many good legal forms and software products at office supply stores and on the Internet (such as www.legalzoom.com) that let you cheaply create a will.

You should get an attorney to write your will if you have a lot of property, complicated business affairs, and/or many children or dependants.

The chapter also contains a review of seven highly recommended books on death and dying.

FINAL INSTRUCTIONS AND DIRECTIVES TO MY SURVIVORS, LOVED ONES, AND FAMILY

By: _____
(printed name)

_____
(signature)

_____
(date)

_____
(address)

_____
(address)

THESE ARE MY FINAL INSTRUCTIONS AND DIRECTIVES IN CASE OF MY SERIOUS ILLNESS OR DEATH

I.   PERSONAL INFORMATION

My full name (and any other names I may have had):

_____

Full name of my spouse/partner:

_____

Full name(s) of my closest living family members to contact in case of my serious illness or death

_____
(name; city/state; phone and/or e-mail)

_____
(name; city/state; phone and/or e-mail)

_____
(name; city/state; phone and/or e-mail)

_____
(name; city/state; phone and/or e-mail)

_____
(name; city/state; phone and/or e-mail)

Full name(s) of my children and/or dependants:

_____
(name; city/state; phone and/or e-mail)

_____
(name; city/state; phone and/or e-mail)

_____
(name; city/state; phone and/or e-mail)

_____
(name; city/state; phone and/or e-mail)

_____
(name; city/state; phone and/or e-mail)

_____
(name; city/state; phone and/or e-mail)

Pets

I have _____ pets, who are:

_____
name/species-breed/age/chipcoded/special needs/veterinary

_____
name/species-breed/age/chipcoded/special needs/veterinary

_____
name/species-breed/age/chipcoded/special needs/veterinary

_____
name/species-breed/age/chipcoded/special needs/veterinary

Please care for each of my pets in case of an emergency or my death, as follows

Full name(s) of close friends to contact in case of my serious illness or death

_____
(name; city/state; phone and/or e-mail)

_____
(name; city/state; phone and/or e-mail)

_____
(name; city/state; phone and/or e-mail)

_____
(name; city/state; phone and/or e-mail)

_____
(name; city/state; phone and/or e-mail)

_____
(name; city/state; phone and/or e-mail)

_____
(name; city/state; phone and/or e-mail)

_____
(name; city/state; phone and/or e-mail)

_____
(name; city/state; phone and/or e-mail)

Other important contacts:

Doctors

_____
name/address/phone or e-mail

_____
name/address/phone or e-mail

_____
name/address/phone or e-mail

_____
name/address/phone or e-mail

Pharmacist

_____
name/address/phone or e-mail

Local hospital

_____
name/address/phone or e-mail

Dentist

_____
name/address/phone or e-mail

Other caregivers

_____
name/address/phone or e-mail

_____
name/address/phone or e-mail

_____
name/address/phone or e-mail

Religious leaders/members

_____
name/address/phone or e-mail

_____
name/address/phone or e-mail

Home help/cleaning

_____
name/address/phone or e-mail

_____
name/address/phone or e-mail

Meal Delivery Providers

_____

name/address/phone or e-mail

Alarm providers (emergency/break-in)

_____

name/address/phone or e-mail

_____

name/address/phone or e-mail

Employment

_____

name/address/phone or e-mail

_____

name/address/phone or e-mail

_____

name/address/phone or e-mail

Volunteer work

_____
name/address/phone or e-mail

_____
name/address/phone or e-mail

_____
name/address/phone or e-mail

Business partner(s)

_____
name/address/phone or e-mail

_____
name/address/phone or e-mail

_____
name/address/phone or e-mail

School/other organizations

_____
name/address/phone or e-mail

Attorney(s) / Lawyer(s)

_____
name/address/phone or e-mail

_____
name/address/phone or e-mail

_____
name/address/phone or e-mail

Home Deliveries/Services:

Mail/courier

Groceries

Newspaper(s)

Gardeners/Yard

Other

II.   FINANCIAL

Current bank and other financial accounts, including savings-checking accounts, CD, mutual funds, 401(k):

_____

institution name / address / account info and #

_____

institution name / address / account info and #

_____

institution name / address / account info and #

_____

institution name / address / account info and #

_____

institution name / address / account info and #

_____

institution name / address / account info and #

_____

institution name / address / account info and #

institution name / address / account info and #

institution name / address / account info and #

institution name / address / account info and #

institution name / address / account info and #

institution name / address / account info and #

institution name / address / account info and #

institution name / address / account info and #

institution name / address / account info and #

Mortgage(s) and home equity credit to be paid:

_____
institution name / address / account info and #

_____
institution name / address / account info and #

_____
institution name / address / account info and #

_____
institution name / address / account info and #

_____
institution name / address / account info and #

_____
institution name / address / account info and #

_____
institution name / address / account info and #

Credit cards and store account cards to be paid:

_____
institution name / address / account info and #

_____
institution name / address / account info and #

_____
institution name / address / account info and #

_____
institution name / address / account info and #

_____
institution name / address / account info and #

_____
institution name / address / account info and #

_____
institution name / address / account info and #

institution name / address / account info and #

institution name / address / account info and #

institution name / address / account info and #

institution name / address / account info and #

institution name / address / account info and #

institution name / address / account info and #

institution name / address / account info and #

institution name / address / account info and #

Other debts to be paid

Pension(s)

_____
institution name / address / account info and #

_____
institution name / address / account info and #

_____
institution name / address / account info and #

_____
institution name / address / account info and #

_____
institution name / address / account info and #

_____
institution name / address / account info and #

_____
institution name / address / account info and #

Other Investments

Stock/Bond and other brokerage accounts

_____
institution name / address / account info and #

_____
institution name / address / account info and #

_____
institution name / address / account info and #

_____
institution name / address / account info and #

_____
institution name / address / account info and #

_____
institution name / address / account info and #

_____
institution name / address / account info and #

Other financial accounts or assets (including real estate owned and safe deposit boxes)

_____
name / address / account info and #

_____
name / address / account info and #

_____
name / address / account info and #

_____
name / address / account info and #

_____
name / address / account info and #

_____
name / address / account info and #

_____
name / address / account info and #

Life Insurance/annuities

_____
institution name / address / account info and #

_____
institution name / address / account info and #

_____
institution name / address / account info and #

Health insurance

_____
institution name / address / account info and #

_____
institution name / address / account info and #

_____
institution name / address / account info and #

Home and property insurance

_____
institution name / address / account info and #

_____
institution name / address / account info and #

_____
institution name / address / account info and #

Car insurance

_____
institution name / address / account info and #

_____
institution name / address / account info and #

_____
institution name / address / account info and #

Other insurance

---
institution name / address / account info and #

---
institution name / address / account info and #

---
institution name / address / account info and #

Utility providers

water/sewer

gas

electricity

landline phone(s)

cell/mobile phone

internet supplier(s)

cable/satellite TV

Rents to be paid to landlord(s) or for storage

_____
name / address / account info and #

_____
name / address / account info and #

_____
name / address / account info and #

Dues to be paid (club memberships; home owner associations; condo dues; etc.)

_____
name / address / account info and #

_____
name / address / account info and #

_____
name / address / account info and #

Government benefits

Social Security

VA

Other

Standing or automated financial orders, including stock/bond sale-purchase orders, direct debits, direct deposits, automatic withdrawals.

_____
name institution / address / order info and account #

_____
name institution / address / order info and account #

_____
name institution / address / order info and account #

_____
name institution / address / order info and account #

_____
name institution / address / order info and account #

_____
name institution / address / order info and account #

III. DOCUMENTS

[describe where these documents are located]

Birth certificate

Marriage/civil partnership certificate(s)

Passport/ travel, resident, or immigration ID, papers, or cards

Deed(s) and mortgage(s) to properties

Driver's license

Social Security card

Last Will & Testament

Trust(s)

Power(s) of attorney

Living will (advance directive; medical power of attorney; pain management plan)

Funeral plan

Other important documents

IV.   PROPERTY

Primary residential real estate property

_____
location / address

Other real estate property for personal use (including timeshare)

_____
location / address

_____
location / address

_____
location / address

_____
location / address

Car(s) / Boat(s) / Other vehicle(s)

_____
location / address

_____
location / address

_____
location / address

_____
location / address

_____
location / address

Location of keys/codes to properties, vaults, vehicles, bank safety boxes (*note: each key/code/card should have a tag to identify what property, vault, vehicle, or box is accessed by the key, code, or card*)

_____
location/address/relation to which property, vault, etc.

_____
location/address/relation to which property, vault, etc.

_____
location/address/relation to which property, vault, etc.

Other important or valuable property

_____
location / address

_____
location / address

_____
location / address

_____
location / address

V. FINAL WISHES

Viewing Arrangements

Should your loved ones ask for a 1-3 hour delay (or more) to view your body before it is taken away for cremation, burial, study, or donation?

Initial one below

_____ YES

_____ NO

If you have any preference, where should your body rest before the funeral? [e.g., at the funeral home, at my home, or other suitable location for viewing by close loved ones]

Cremation

If cremated, I want my ashes to be:

Initial and complete one below

_____ buried at _____
(address)

_____ stored with _____
(name, address, phone)

Memorial and Funeral Service

I want my memorial or celebration-of-life service to be held, as follows:

Initial one below

_____ None / whatever my loved ones want

_____ At same time as my funeral / burial

_____ Pursuant to my religious
affiliation, which is

_____

With the following persons to conduct, direct, lead, speak at, or participate in the service

_____ Funeral home

_____ Other, as follows

_____

_____

I want my funeral or burial service to be held, as follows:

Initial one below

_____ None / whatever my loved ones want

_____ Pursuant to my religious
affiliation, which is

_____

With the following persons to conduct, direct, lead, speak at, or participate in the service

_____ Other, as follows

_____

_____

_____

The following person(s) cannot be excluded from, and must be invited and allowed to attend, my memorial service, celebration-of-life service, funeral service and/or burial service:

_____

name/address/phone or e-mail

_____

name/address/phone or e-mail

_____

name/address/phone or e-mail

_____

name/address/phone or e-mail

_____

name/address/phone or e-mail

_____

name/address/phone or e-mail

Burial grave/crypt location

Initial one below

_____ I have a burial plot located at:

_____
(address)

_____ I do not have a burial plot but would prefer one located at:

_____
(address)

Flowers / donations at my memorial and/or funeral

Initial one below

_____ I have NO preference if people want to provide flowers and/or make donations to charitable causes

_____ I prefer for people to provide flowers

_____ I prefer if people make donations to charitable causes, including:

_____
(name and address)

SEVEN HIGHLY RECOMMENDED BOOKS
ON SERIOUS ILLNESS, DEATH, AND DYING

The Complete Bedside Companion
by Rodger McFarlane

> A comprehensive and very practical guide for end-of-life caregivers. Written by an experienced hospice expert. Includes excellent tips on how to physically care for the seriously ill and what to say to the dying.

More Than A Parting Prayer
by William H. Griffith.

> Very helpful spiritual guide for end-of-life caregivers. Written by an experienced and sensitive hospice chaplain. Includes excellent guidance on what to say and do for the dying and how to help everyone prepare for death, including the caregiver.

The Needs of the Dying
by David Kessler

> Useful guide written by experienced and compassionate advocate. Identifies and thoughtfully discusses seven key areas of concern: the need to be treated as a living human being; the need for hope; the need to express emotions; the need to participate in care; the need for honesty; the need for spirituality; and, the need to be free of physical pain.

At Home with Dying
by Merrill Collett

> Practical and spiritual tips for caregivers who are caring for the dying at home. Regardless of your beliefs, you will be helped by the Buddhist Zen approach written by a hospice worker at the San Francisco Zen Hospice Project, which has helped thousands of dying individuals and their loved ones.

Comfort and Care in a Final Illness
by June Cerza Kolf

A well-written and very practical guide on how the sick and caregivers can prepare for the end of life with hope and intelligence. Written by experienced hospice provider.

Jane Brody's Guide to the Great Beyond
by Jane Brody

A practical guide on how the sick and caregivers can prepare medically, legally, and emotionally for the end of life

On Angel's Eve
by Garnette Arledge

A compassionate spiritual guide for end-of-life caregivers. Written by an experienced and sensitive hospice chaplain. Includes guidance from several major religions on what to say and do to comfort and support the dying.

FURTHER READING

Planning A Good Death
written by BBC editors

A brief (32 pages) practical, sensitive, and intelligent guide to planning in case of one's death. Although written for British audiences, it is perfectly useful in any country. Attractively printed, easy to read and understand, and made available for free on the Internet by the BBC.

Available for free at
www.scribd.com/doc/13645892/Folger-BBC

Made in the USA
Lexington, KY
23 October 2015